Take my words as loving advice,
because I want only the best for you.
Take my love with you
wherever you go in this world.
It has been and always will be yours.

— Sandra Sturtz Hauss

For an Extra-Special TEEN

Words to Help You Strive, Thrive, and

Make This WORLD Yours!

A Blue Mountain Arts® Collection
Edited by Diane Mastromarino

Blue Mountain Press™

Boulder, Colorado

The publisher wishes to acknowledge and thank Virginia Nowell for creating the illustrations that appear in this book, as well as the Blue Mountain Arts creative staff.

We wish to thank Susan Polis Schutz for permission to reprint the following poems that appear in this publication: "You are such an outstanding person…" and "There is a fine line between…." Copyright © 1991 by Stephen Schutz and Susan Polis Schutz. And for "This life is yours…" Copyright © 1978 by Continental Publications. All rights reserved.

Library of Congress Control Number: 2003105118
ISBN: 0-88396-750-2

ACKNOWLEDGMENTS appear on page 64.

Certain trademarks are used under license.

Manufactured in the United States of America.
First Printing: 2003

This book is printed on recycled paper.

This book is printed on fine quality, laid embossed, 80 lb. paper. This paper has been specially produced to be acid free (neutral pH) and contains no groundwood or unbleached pulp. It conforms with all the requirements of the American National Standards Institute, Inc., so as to ensure that this book will last and be enjoyed by future generations.

Blue Mountain Arts, Inc.

P.O. Box 4549, Boulder, Colorado 80306

Contents
(Authors listed in order of first appearance)

THIS WORLD IS YOURS

As you **go on** in this world
keep looking **forward** to the **future**
to **all** you might be
Don't let old **mistakes**
or **misfortunes** hold you down:
learn from them, **forgive** yourself
— or others — and **move on.**
Do not be bothered
or discouraged by **adversity.**
Instead meet it as a **challenge.**
Be **empowered** by the courage it takes you
to overcome obstacles. **Learn things.**
Learn something **new** every day.

Be interested in others
and what they might teach you.
But do not look for yourself
in the faces of others.
Do not look for who you are
in other people's approval.
As far as who you are
and who you will become goes —
the answer is always within yourself.
Believe in yourself.
Follow your heart and your dreams.
You — like everyone else —
will make mistakes.
But as long as you are true to the strength
within your own heart… you can never go wrong.

— Ashley Rice

REMEMBER THIS...

Sometimes it isn't easy
growing up.
The world
   isn't always
      fair to you.
In the tough times of life...
when the days aren't going
the way you'd like them to...
I want you to remember
that you can
   always
      turn to me.

REMEMBER ME...

I want to be a place
you can come to for shelter,
for unconditional caring,
for sharing
   all the support
      one can give.
I want to be a person
you can turn to for answers
and understanding,
or just to reinforce
the feeling of how
   incredibly special
      you are.

— Douglas Pagels

I can't rock you in my arms,
read you stories,
   or tuck you into bed anymore.

But I still think

the world of you.

And I long to find a way
to tell you how much
I will always love you.

— Paula Holmes-Eber

Sometimes I look at you
and I still see a vision
of the child you once were...
a smile surrounded by
chocolate ice cream,
knees covered with
scrapes and bruises,
feet that never stopped moving,
always carrying you from
one adventure to the next.
It's amazing to stand back
and realize how much you've grown...
my child, no longer a child,
all grown-up and ready
to face the world.

— Carol Thomas

From Me...
WISHES and WANTS

 I want you to be safe and smart and cautious.

 I want you to be wise beyond your years.

 I don't want you to grow up too fast.

 I want you to come to me with your fears.

 I want the people who share your days to realize that they are in the presence of a very special someone.

 I want you to know that opportunities will come, and you'll have many goals to achieve.

For You...
HOPES and PRAYERS

 I hope you'll get your feet wet with new experiences, but be careful never to get in over your head.

 I hope you realize how capable you are and that your possibilities are unlimited.

 I hope you never lose your childlike wonder, your delight and appreciation in interesting things.

 I pray that you won't rush the future and that you'll slowly build on the steppingstones of the past.

 You have a strong foundation of family and friends and joy that will always last wherever you go in this world.

— Douglas Pagels

In between the joy of being
a protected, cherished child
and the contentment of being
a free, independent adult...

is the fun

the frustration

the confusion

the boredom

the excitement

the despondency

and the elation

of being a teenager.

— Barbara Cage

The **freedom** that comes
with adulthood also comes with
a lot of **responsibility.**
People treat you like **a child**
in some ways but expect you to act
like **an adult** in others.
All you can do is your **best.**
Follow your heart
and use **common sense.**
Most of all, believe in yourself
and in your **dreams.**
You will likely have to make
some **sacrifices,**
but dreams are worth the effort.
Make time to **enjoy** yourself,
but **work hard,** too.
You'll find that the **present**
and the **future** will be all you could
ever **hope** for.

— Barbara Cage

BE TRUE...

Throughout life
you will walk many paths
meet many people
and experience many things
Don't ever try to change
the person you are
to meet someone else's needs
Be yourself —
Never stop caring about
the things you value in life
and never stop striving to be
    your best

— Deana Marino

...TO YOU

You are such an **outstanding** person
and I hope nothing ever changes
your **inner beauty**

As you keep growing
remember always
to look at things the way you do now —
with **sensitivity**
honesty
compassion
and a touch of **innocence**
Remember that people and situations
may not **always** be
as they appear
but if you remain **true** to yourself
things will be all right

— Susan Polis Schutz

Never Fear
Being Your Best

Sing to the stars;
tell them your **secrets.**

Dream great dreams
and don't be afraid
to chase them...

Live **boldly**. Love **passionately**.
Stand on your toes
   and **tickle** the sky.
Throw yourself into the world;
Be **brave** but not foolish.
Expect no more from others
Than you are **willing** to give.
Be **generous** with your talents,
   your time,
     and your **heart**.

Never fear being your **best**;
Know that to me you already are.
Above all, know this:
Should ever you fall,
My **love** will catch you
   and bring you **safely** home.

— Kathy Larson

Remember What Is Most Important...

It's not having **everything** go right;
it's **facing** whatever goes wrong.
It's not being without fear;
it's having the **determination**
    to go on in spite of it.
It's not where you stand,
but the **direction** you're going in.
It's **believing** you have already
been given everything
    you need to **handle** life.
It's not being able to rid
the **world** of all its injustices;
it's being able to **rise** above them.

It's the belief in your heart
that there will always be
more good than bad in the world.
Remember to live just this one day
and not add tomorrow's troubles
   to today's load.
Remember that every day ends
and brings a new tomorrow
full of exciting new things.
Love what you do,
   do the best you can,
and always remember
   how much you are loved.

— Vickie M. Worsham

Every day...
is a new day,
a new chance to succeed.

Every day...
should be honored
for the blessing it is.

Every day...
is a time for courage
and achievement,
everything from spending the day
"making it happen"
to simply remembering
that all those horizons
that sometimes seem so distant
aren't really so very far.

— Collin McCarty

Mistakes

are

steppingstones

upon which we build our future.

With each one

we gain insight and courage,

learn something new,

and

rise a little closer

to the sunshine.

Then we begin again.

— Elle Mastro

Live Your Life... Learning

Learning is not
just about teachers,
textbooks, and tests.
It is not just going to class,
memorizing facts,
and raising your hand
as often as you can.
Learning is about
the joy of discovery
and the mastery
of meeting challenges.
It is the gift
of self-determination —
a gift for your mind, body,
and spirit...
the gift you need to make
your dreams happen.

— Jacqueline Schiff

Experience
something new
every day.

Learn from the world
around you...
from the words you read,
the sounds you hear,
the touches you feel,
and the faces
you see.

In the course of your daily tasks,
search for
new perspectives,
lean toward understanding,
and make
the commonplace
a wondrous place to be.

Make your happiness...
a **happiness**
that lasts.

— Collin McCarty

Don't strive to impress others;
strive to impress yourself.
Be the person you were meant to be.

E
v
e
r
y
t
h
i
n
g

e
l
s
e

w
i
l
l

f
a
l
l

i
n

l
i
n
e

...and your dreams will come true.

— Karen Poynter Taylor

You know
yourself
better than anyone,
so set your own
limits.
Think your own
thoughts.
Dream
your own
dreams.
Make your own plans.
Do
your own
thing.
Be yourself.
Be the
best
you can be
and
accept
that as enough.

— Donna Fargo

Never Lose Faith in Yourself

Never think that any part of you
Is lacking.
Never doubt your abilities.
Never question your judgment.
Never let anyone or anything
Make you feel less than you are,
Because who you are
    Is someone special.

Never feel that the next step
Is a step too far.
If you're stumbling as you walk,
Hold your head high and
Know that no other person's
Words or actions
Can ever hurt you,
Because who you are
    Is someone special.

Never lose faith in yourself.
Just look around you —
At the friends who surround you —
Because they love and care for you,
Support you,
And believe in you...
    Because you are someone special.

— Ashley Bell

Always Be True

Be true... to your dreams, and keep them alive. Never let anyone change your mind about what you feel you can achieve. Always believe in yourself.

Be true... to the light that is deep within you. Hold on to your faith, hope, and joy for life. Keep good thoughts in your mind and good feelings in your heart. Be giving, forgiving, patient, and kind. Have faith in yourself. Be your own best friend, and listen to the voice that tells you to be your best self.

Be true... to yourself in the paths that you choose. Follow your talents and passions, and never forget that there is no brighter light than the one within you.

— Jacqueline Schiff

You Can Do...

If anyone tries to tell you
that you can't work hard enough
to face the task in front of you...
show them that you're tough.

If anyone tries to tell you
that you are not that strong,
don't listen to discouragement...
know that you belong.

...Anything!

If anyone tries to tell you that
you can't sing your own song
or make your way in the world...

La La La

prove them wrong.

— Ashley Rice

Understand Success...

Success is the satisfaction of knowing that I did my best, I gave my all, then releasing the outcome to the universe. Success is trusting that what is to be will be and that if there's anything else I should do about it, it will be made known to me.

Success is not giving up, even though I've failed a thousand times. It's finding another angle or fresh approach that allows me to try again with the hope that this will be the time I'll reach my goal, for it's knowing that unless I try again, I may lose my opportunity.

…and Go for It!

Success is someone saying "thank you" for something I did and communicating the feeling of true appreciation. It is having someone to love and be loved by. Success is having a roof over my head, food to eat, a telephone, and a car to drive.

Success is being hopeful and communicating hope to another human being, helping someone up some hill in life. It's that nudge at just the right time, that little bit of advice or encouragement that whispers in someone's ear to carry on and not give up.

Success is knowing that success is not everything.

— Donna Fargo

When the days come that
are filled with frustration
and unexpected responsibilities,

REMEMBER THIS...

Believe in yourself
and all you want your life to be,
because the challenges
  and changes
will only help you to find
the dreams that you know
are meant to come true for you.

— Deanna Beisser

When your day is blue
I will bring a yellow paintbrush

When your heart feels broken
I will always have bandages

When you need to be quiet
I will sit with you in silence

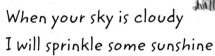

When your sky is cloudy
I will sprinkle some sunshine

When the mountain seems steep
I will push you uphill

When you can't help but cry
I will pack extra tissues

Whatever you need...
   I will always be there

    — Elle Mastro

Climb Up High

Don't
let life
pass you by;
the only way
to get ahead is to
hold your head up high.
Try not to be discouraged
when things get in your way;
just climb each mountain inch
by inch, and take life day by day.
Eventually you will find the strength
you had to seek, not only to scale that
mountain but reach its mighty peak.

— Tracy Nash

TRY AND TRY... AND TRY

If you ever feel like giving up...

DON'T.

If you think you can't do something...

TRY.

If you try and fail...

THEN TRY AGAIN.

If you don't, you may always wonder why you gave up so easily. Believe in whatever you think is worth believing in, and never stop until you feel you have done all that you can to secure your dreams. I have such faith in you, and I know that you are capable of achieving anything you want.

ALWAYS REMEMBER THAT.

— Tracy Nash

The glory
is not in
never falling...

...but in rising
every time
you fail.

— Chinese Proverb

If you back away
from **obstacles**
that appear before you
because they seem too **difficult,**
then you're not
being **true** to yourself.

Don't be afraid to take
risks, or even to fail.
It isn't about **winning** or **losing.**
It's about **loving** yourself enough
and believing in who you are
that **counts** in the end.

— Tracy Nash

You Have What It Takes...

Winners take chances.
Like everyone else, they fear failing,
but they **refuse** to let fear
control them.
They **don't** give up.
When life gets rough, they **hang on**
until the going gets better.
They are **flexible.**
They realize there is more than one way
and are willing to try others.
Winners know they are not **perfect.**
They **respect** their weaknesses
while making the most of their **strengths.**
They fall, but they **don't** stay down.
They stubbornly refuse to let a fall
keep them from **climbing.**

...to Be a Winner

Winners are **positive** thinkers
who see **good** in all things.
From the ordinary, they make
the **extraordinary.**
Winners believe in the path
they have chosen
even when it's **hard,**
even when others can't see
where they are going.
Winners are **patient.**
They know a goal is only as worthy
as the effort that's required
to **achieve** it.
Winners are people like you.
They make this **world**
a **better** place to be.

— Nancye Sims

This life is yours
Take the power
to choose what you want to do
and do it well

Take the power
to love what you want in life
and love it honestly

Take the power
to walk in the forest
and be a part of nature

Take the power
to control your own life
No one else can do this for you
Nothing is too good for you
You deserve the best

Take the power
to make your life
healthy
exciting and worthwhile

The time is now
Take the power
to create a successful
happy
life

— Susan Polis Schutz

How to be...

a rock star,
prizewinner, teacher,
astrophysicist, novelist,
professional wrestler, actor,
painter, radio personality,
editor, filmmaker,
guitar-player, columnist,
astronaut, singer, designer,
cartoonist, inventor,
architect, builder, producer,
writer, athlete, artist,
programmer, dancer,
technician, or stylist
in one step or less...

go for it.

— Ashley Rice

There is inside you all of the potential to be
whatever you want to be.

Imagine
yourself

as you

would like

to be,

doing what

you want to do,

and each day,

take

one step

toward your

dream.

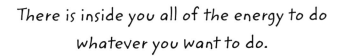

There is inside you all of the energy to do
whatever you want to do.

— Donna Levine Small

I want to share
these thoughts
with you...

(even though I hope you already know them)

Your sense of humor
delights me.

Your laughter is
one of my favorite sounds.

Your smile lights up my heart.

People know they can
count on you.

You're helpful to others,
and you are independent, as well.

Being your parent has been
one of my GREATEST joys.

— Barbara Cage

A VERY SPECIAL WISH LIST...

I wish I could tell you that people
won't hurt your feelings...
But they will.

I wish that you would listen to me
when I tell you something for your
own good and for your safety...
I hope.

I wish for you to realize that
all the other kids feel just as
nervous and worried as you do...
I promise.

I wish that you could know that not
everyone who says they do
actually does...
They don't.

…FOR AN EXTRA-SPECIAL TEENAGER

I wish that I could wrap you in angel's wings
and hold your heart in my pocket
so no one can break it…
But I can't.

I wish I could cry your tears,
and lead your way,
and heal your hurts…
But you must.

I wish I could lessen the weight
of peer pressure from your heart…
I'll try.

I wish for you to know that I love you,
and I am proud of the person
you are choosing to become…
I am.

— Cynthia Dite Sirni

My dreams
for your life
might not always
be the same ones
you seek.

BUT ONE THING REMAINS THE SAME:

Your happiness
will always be
my greatest
treasure
in this world.

— Nancy Gilliam

There is a fine line between
a parent telling her child
too much
or too little…

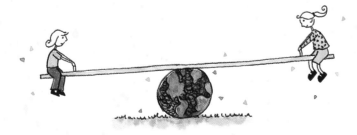

…I hope I have struck
a proper balance

— Susan Polis Schutz

WORDS OF WISDOM...

 Always take time for...

Big smiles. Sunday mornings. Long walks. Warm appreciation.
Precious memories. Things that bring a sense of joy to
your heart. Staying in touch... with the people who will
always mean so much.

 Find a way to...

Be good to yourself. (Really good.) Build the bridges that
will take you everywhere you've ever wanted to go. Write
out your own definition of success, and then do your
absolute best to make that story come true. Get closer
and closer to the summit of every mountain you've ever
wanted to climb. Make the most... of your moment... of
this moment in time.

...FOR A WORLD OF HAPPINESS

 ## Make plans to...

Slow down the days. Find your perfect pace. Be strong enough. Be gentle enough. Reap the sweet rewards that will come from all the good things you do and all the great things you give. Keep things in perspective.

 ## Remember to...

Invest wisely in the best riches of all. Share invaluable words over warm cups in quiet places. Treasure time spent in heart-to-heart conversations. Laugh a lot. Work it all out. Move ahead of every worry. Move beyond any sorrows. Have yourself a wealth of beautiful tomorrows.

— Douglas Pagels

Many days go by
and I find myself saying
the same things to you
day in and day out:

Clean your room.
Is your room clean?
Do your homework.
Did you finish your homework?
Don't be late.
Take out the trash, please.

Many nights,
after you have fallen asleep
and look so peaceful
I have wondered to myself:

Did I tell you that I love you?
That I appreciate all you do for me?
That through your entire life
you will find me
in your cheering section?

Always remember that, I love you very much,
and I am proud of all that you do
and all that you stand for.

— Toni Crossgrove Shippen

In your **happiest**
and most **exciting** moments...
my heart will celebrate and smile
   beside you.

In your **lowest** lows,
my love will be there to keep you warm,
to give you **strength**...
and to remind you that your sunshine
   is sure to come again.

In your moments of **accomplishment**,
I will be filled so full of **pride**...
that I may have a hard time keeping
   the feeling inside me.

In your moments of **disappointment,**
I will be a **shoulder** to cry on,
a **hand** to hold, and a **love**...
that will gently enfold you
    until everything's okay.

In your **gray** days, I will help you
search, one by one...
    for the colors of the rainbow.

In your **bright** and **shining** hours,
I will be **smiling,** too...
    right along beside you.

— Laurel Atherton

It has been a marvelous adventure
watching you emerge
into the beautiful person you are —
like a caterpillar evolves
    into a dazzling butterfly.

But to tell you the truth,
I can't wait to see the person
you continue to become,
because I have a feeling that,
with you, the best is yet to come.

— Donna Gephart

I see you
for all that you once were
for all that you are now
and for all that you
someday will be —
a precious gift
a loving heart
and a blessing to the lives
of all that come to know you

— Deana Marino

CHOOSE WISELY...

I *hope* you'll choose happiness
   when at all possible.
I *hope* you'll keep good memories
   and discard hurts and failures.
I *hope* you'll allow yourself
      to make mistakes
and realize that's when we learn
      our biggest lessons.
You are a precious and valued person
who deserves the best in life —
take it, and share it with others.

— Barbara Cage

...AND WATCH YOUR LIFE SOAR

You have what it takes
to make a **difference**
in this **world**.
Look for goodness,
dream big,
and **believe** in your heart
that who you are
is all that you need.
Work, play, dream,
and keep your perspective
no matter what comes your way.
Reward yourself often;
paint your own **rainbows.**
Be your own hero,
be your own **guide.**
Let your **imagination** run free
and **watch** your life **soar.**

— Linda E. Knight

THIS WORLD IS YOURS

In this world,
there is only one
You.

You have your
very own ways.

You've got your own
walking shoes
in this world.

You are the
only one who
smiles and laughs
exactly as you do.

You are the
only one who lives
and thinks exactly
as you do.

You are your
very own you.

You've got your
own dreams and
your ideas, too…

You can make
them come true…
because
this world is yours.

— Ashley Rice

ACKNOWLEDGMENTS

We gratefully acknowledge the permission granted by the following authors, publishers, and authors' representatives to reprint poems or excerpts from their publications.

Sandra Sturtz Hauss for "Take my words as loving advice...." Copyright © 2003 by Sandra Sturtz Hauss. All rights reserved.

Paula Holmes-Eber for "I can't rock you in my arms...." Copyright © 2003 by Paula Holmes-Eber. All rights reserved.

Barbara Cage for "In between the joy of being...," "The freedom that comes with adulthood...," and "I hope you'll choose happiness...." Copyright © 2003 by Barbara Cage. All rights reserved.

Kathy Larson for "Sing to the stars...." Copyright © 2003 by Kathy Larson. All rights reserved.

Vickie M. Worsham for "It's not having everything go right...." Copyright © 2003 by Vickie M. Worsham. All rights reserved.

Jacqueline Schiff for "Learning is not just about teachers...." Copyright © 2003 by Jacqueline Schiff. All rights reserved.

PrimaDonna Entertainment Corp. for "You know yourself better than..." and "Success is the satisfaction of knowing..." by Donna Fargo. Copyright © 1999 by PrimaDonna Entertainment Corp. All rights reserved.

Ashley Bell for "Never think that any part of you is lacking." Copyright © 2003 by Ashley Bell. All rights reserved.

Cynthia Dite Sirni for "I wish I could tell you that...." Copyright © 2003 by Cynthia Dite Sirni. All rights reserved.

Donna Gephart for "It has been a marvelous adventure...." Copyright © 2003 by Donna Gephart. All rights reserved.

Linda E. Knight for "You have what it takes...." Copyright © 2003 by Linda E. Knight. All rights reserved.

A careful effort has been made to trace the ownership of selections used in this anthology in order to obtain permission to reprint copyrighted material and give proper credit to the copyright owners. If any error or omission has occurred, it is completely inadvertent, and we would like to make corrections in future editions provided that written notification is made to the publisher:

BLUE MOUNTAIN ARTS, INC., P.O. Box 4549, Boulder, Colorado 80306.